TUA FORSSTRÖM

SNOW L

TRANSLATED BY DAVID McDUFF

BLOODAXE BOOKS

ISBN: 1 85224 111 X

First published 1990 by
Bloodaxe Books Ltd,
P.O. Box 1SN,
Newcastle upon Tyne NE99 1SN.

Bloodaxe Books Ltd acknowledges
the financial assistance of Northern Arts.

ACKNOWLEDGEMENTS
David McDuff wishes to thank Suomalaisen Kirjallisuuden
Seura, Helsinki, for their translation grant.
This book is a translation of *Snöleopard* by Tua Forsström,
first published by Söderström & C:o Förlagsaktiebolag,
Helsinki, in 1987. Thanks are due to Söderströms
and to Leif Rosas for the back cover photograph.
Some of these translations have previously appeared
in *Books from Finland, Scandinavian Review* and *Stand*.

David McDuff is one of Britain's leading translators of Scandinavian and Russian literature. He has translated works of fiction by Dostoyevsky, Tolstoy and Leskov in the Penguin Classics series, and four other books for Bloodaxe: Irina Ratushinskaya's *No, I'm Not Afraid*, the *Complete Poems* of Edith Södergran, *Selected Poems* by Marina Tsvetayeva, and the Finland-Swedish poetry anthology *Ice Around Our Lips*.

Printed in Great Britain by
Bell & Bain Limited, Glasgow, Scotland.

One never swims out into the same water
In the light night waits immediately below
One falls like a leaf through the space
of seconds, a wind blows
darkness against your cheek.

I

There is a certain kind of loss
and September's objectivity

Something is released imperceptibly,
and is displaced: it does not

matter. There is a coolness
that has settled on the surfaces,

it kept me calm. One sits
on a bench that looks like other benches,

trains leave on time, dogs bark,
one is. Close to you

I read books and confused my name
with names of other places: a summer kitchen

with radio news in front of blowing curtains,
the cousin sailing in the bay

I stood on the threshold of my mother's
bedroom, she was not there

Bedrooms smell differently in summer:
a weather of gentle snowfalls

One sees a snake and treads carefully
on the grass for a few days   Still weakened

by revenge: I inform against myself. There was
a magic room called Childhood

and always the same alien particulars
I have kept calm for a long time. And now

the wind takes hold of the sail
and drives my cousin straight across the bay

the small red sail red against the green

Foliage mirrored in the eye, the broken neck
describes what it's like to be a bird and fly
towards foliage mirrored in the shiny heavens:
a confused memory of the joy in rushing
to one's rendezvous with someone so like oneself.

In the photographs your
eyes are a shade
asymmetrical, there is
no formula for
human beings. Water
and light strangely distributed
Infractions, imagination.
Nakedness. Innocence and crime.
The rondo flows from one of the
inner rooms: something completed
and inevitable
'In order to be able to live in the world
one must first lay its foundation.'
I slit open an envelope
with a knife, freshly mown grass
steams in through the window
It's the suddenness!
In slow processes!
I say that I regret everything
I regret almost everything, it
makes no difference
I have known you since I was a
child and thought like a child
Yes, water and light.
Cracks in the socle.
Inflammations.

Juvena Skin Concentrate
on face and throat.
There is something that is preparing
its departure, fussing with foreign
currency, mumblingly trying
to attract attention.
But everything's all right, I say!
Over the pines in the west the sky is on fire.
Juvena Hydroactive Care
on temples and throat.

It is the way it is.
It may seem
hopeless.
It is hopeless.
Act only according
to the instructions, avoid
hysteria. Avoid
anorexia nervosa. At first
one cries a lot, doesn't want
to be a mistake and the Flowers of
Evil. One begins to feel better.
Someone stretched out
naked and didn't want to.
Someone let it happen.
One acknowledges receipt of parcels
that contain darkness quarried
from darkness in another place.
One reports oneself missing.
One reports oneself damaged.
I held someone tightly
in my mouth until it
flowed over.

It was like pouring water over a peacock.
Wandering through the basement of a nightclub looking for
someone long since forgotten.
A footprint in dried clay.
An impotent mathematical formula.
It was like making an invitation to the waltz while stumbling
forward on crutches.
'Foolish, Sir! Each year you stubbornly persist
in visiting this Imaginary Festival, This Vale
of Tears, These Loathsome Springs. At the last moment
you ask to postpone your departure. This
happens without fail. Without fail you sink
back into brooding about life's glowing days of
windfall. You will probably always re-
turn empty-handed. Won't you?'

Clouds of sand and litter blow upwards.

Perhaps some day one will emerge on the other side, in the cool reading rooms

Someone is spilling me out like water.

We request the speedy settlement of the
following matter: the house with the closed
shutters. That noise goes on all round the clock
these days: wailing, laughter, the sound of Fiddler
Olle being danced and a monotonous mumbling.
We are normal, particularly ordinary people.
It sounds as though heavy objects are being dragged
across the floor. In between there is silence.
We demand silence! Identities,
particulars and a full confession:
that it be proved without delay that they are foreigners.
It is getting dark, it is still snowing, we demand
swift intervention on the council's part.

The Fieldmouse's Prayer

Father, in the blowing greenery of Your summer,
Father, in the endlessly green vault of Your summer:
Help me to get down into the ditch when Your
elect draw near along the road.

Dust swarms in the sunbeam.
On familiar terms with the Divine
you stand at the blackboard, expounding
the movements of the Soul and Love's
effect on the digestion.
You are wearing a pin-stripe suit,
you are handsome. The plainest
of the female students raises
her hand and asks in intense embarrassment
'why one doesn't faint with grief'.
You return to Descartes' Treatise
on the Passions of the Soul, Article XCVII.
From the corridor there is a smell of damp wool.
You look round: pupils dilated with
desire and darkness mirroring their reflection.

They come out at dusk, flat
shadows across the fields. They are composed in equal
parts of pig, badger, fox. Helplessness
is their principal distinguishing mark. They root in the snow
for something to eat. We find them unnatural:
their aimless wandering, their hunger, their obscene
lack of protection. At the first sign of danger the he-martin
lies down and pretends to be dead. We find such behaviour
pitiful, we find the pitiful repulsive, we
are outraged by the hungry shadows of
this sugar-beet field, so unlike the snow leopard that silently
pursues its prey six thousand metres
above sea-level.

Does one get used to them, Claes?
These accident black spots?

Music is order, play
so that the subterranean parts

overwinter, that which is yearning
and prison, Claire de Lune

'Friendship is a loneliness
freed from loneliness's fear'

Does one get used to them, Claes?
These accident black spots?

Months of animosity, the vapour of fever
and distance in the children's breathing

The waterfall, the unceasingly collapsing
wall of tears and interruptions

What's left is perhaps
chance rooms, an uneventful

view of a country road in October.
To play so that something overwinters

us all and the gentle trees
in a season of breaking glass.

There is something about
the taxi-driver's babyish
cheeks that says:
that it exists.
That it really exists.
That a nocturnal music
flows along the ice-cold road.
Yes, there is a glowing point
somewhere for us all where
rags and masks fall.
So that there will never
have been any rags or masks.
There we are eye against eye,
ashes against rain.

To live in its reflection
was sufficient. Rain

streams like silver in June
An entertainment is in progress. We are played out

on an old-fashioned open-air stage
with birch trees, in transformation

I'm homesick. The sense of
lightness in the water

The sense of lightness when one
comes out of the water

One asks someone to come back,
they come back at night

uninvited. Rain streams
against silver-rotting wood

There is always a bit left over

(to Biskops-Arnö)

There is always a bit left over.
In the view here of green-shadowed water, reeds
shadowed by trees, the mud, the crickets...
One must have an Image to retain.
A net of gaudy fishes, a forgotten
book in the grass for the wind
to leaf through. A dancing bear.
One must hold up one's Image
against the subterranean thunder.
One must confess a Weakness:
inflamed eyes, one's love.
Those short journeys can be very long.
In the newspaper contemporaries have begun to die,
even the winters have become strangely imperceptible.
Oh what cheating, Mr Livingstone!
One writes on one's wall: 'They must show that
they have been fools and were as miserable as we are'
Yes, there is a sleep that must be slept,
but first one wants to grow potatoes
and put one's name down for a trip abroad.
It takes time to learn boogie-woogie,
believe me, Sir, it takes time.
There's a wind from the west now
One must be able to reconstruct everything,
things that never happened.

O gall-sores of the soul! The heart's
blisters! Arms around shoulders, bright-clad
friends, giggling in the late evening
on the gravel under the chestnut trees
It takes time to learn something.
In the wind a vapour of lakes and waterweed
What you saw today no one has seen
and you will remember, or forget.
But the first chord remains.

It was in the shadow of the green room
with low windows shadowed by the lime tree's foliage

in the shadow of clouds. It was the kind of day
when animals seek out water

as we seek out springs, the pure
coolness in a loved embrace and cathedrals,

the green rooms under water shadowed
by clouds. 'It's like in physics'

says a schoolchild conducting the world's first
experiment with water, salt and sand

noting in an exercise book: 'An underwater
sandstorm whirls towards the bottom of the vessel'

and that we all consist of the same water, dance
and vertigo, and a few plain coincidences

and something that goes beyond ourselves.
I must stop here. You will certainly

have read many letters on this subject, and are tired.
One wanders from one room to the other

through the days like shadows, clouds.

II

'We in embracing nights,
we fall from closeness to closeness,
and where the loving one melts,
we are a stone that plummets.'

RAINER MARIA RILKE

Thank you for Your kind parcel.
I must, however, return everything:
there are plenty of scissors, stones grow
into mountains, and the chains were too heavy
even for Selma, my cow.
That's enough of the Flowers of Evil, and one
thing and another.
Mother said I was a darling child,
but she has stopped crying.
Sometimes it is spring, and sometimes it is winter.
It was brilliant night, and the courtyard plummeted
like a swarm of shooting-stars through space.
Fire burns more quickly than one thinks.
It's like this: there's a house somewhere,
whoops! there's no house anywhere.
I have seen a photograph of the University.
But where are you at nights?
They found charred newspapers in the snow
right up at the Marsh, I miss
Father and Mother, but one has to be somewhere.
Everyone says I shouldn't have done it.
I have bits of fur and snot in my hair,
one shouldn't get oneself in such a mess.
It's a question of being a good pupil!
A Nebula is a mist of incandescent garbage.
Before, I used to mourn both life and death, ought
I all the same to be sorry about Selma?

They bring the food in on green trays
I am terribly hungry, so I
must eat instead
Mother said I fluttered like a butterfly
over the garden path, but she's not crying now.
Mother raked the garden path beautifully.
It's not nice to eat so much.
It's nice not to be sad any more.
I dreamed that someone unbuttoned my blouse
and rusty iron bled and bled from my mouth
onto the floor. Otherwise everything is fine.

Dear Marilyn Monroe

I have been reading about you in the newspaper again.
You stood outside your house in Beverly Hills
and said you were the sum total of
forty lonely hotel rooms.
You were dressed in provocative attire,
even your hair was radiant as a cloud.
I myself have never stayed in a hotel.
I am writing to you because one ought to avoid
certain people, as far as possible
They need all that they see.
They need you because you are radiant
and like a child. Do you know
what people are saying about the Attorney General?
And also about the President and yourself?
I don't mean to be nosey, believe me
But I am older than you,
and not so good-looking: Between night and dawn
someone will take your life   In the morning
they will go to church with their wife and children
It's none of my business, of course
There is a lot in the newspaper about nerves
What I mean is: you are sort of precious
you are like something in us all
you're forever talking about death, but you have
never been hurled into the deep darkness that drowns
people in night and ashes without mercy

33

So give up dressing half-naked
Don't whisper that funny way when you sing
Give up solitary walks and darkness   Your house
can hardly be seen for all the greenery in the photographs,
are you interested in gardening?

You were right: it's fine here.
What mirror-gleaming floors, reflecting
the shiny crystals in the garden!
Immediately after our arrival we were given
the task of whitewashing the frescoes,
we made it clean and tidy
Here I practise my obedience
I practise my ability to see: the disintegration of
matter, the damp, the fine
cracks, the silence, that everything rots.
If one doesn't immediately prevent it!
If one doesn't constantly putty and paint over!
I don't dare to think that thought: how I used to live
my life in the mire, like a pig!
Every day we set aside four hours for Systematisation
One soon gets used to it, you were right of course
One also gets used to the way time is reckoned
Some of my friends are regrettable exceptions
They copy from forgetfulness at nights
concurrences of the planets, market days,
cattle auctions, the time
when snow that lies arrives.
The duration of the hours of darkness.
I think I ought to report them, I don't know
They talk about strange kinds of birds, and about
the word having power over people's
hearts. A curious belief
The sanitary arrangements are excellent

Another advantage is that one doesn't have to die
I really have nothing to complain of. I
have now completely forgotten the old
geography: all that which was rain, membranes
of fever and salt.

III

PENELOPE

(Cantata)

1.

I am Wife, besieged.
Years flowed like water,
One gets used to it. Sometimes
I would separate from my waiting
And look at my Suitors, deprived of
You. I forgot myself, I forgot
The nights under His hands
As one forgets the dream until
It recurs. Years passed
Like moments. There is
Such waiting that one separates

2.

What we call time
Is perhaps to train oneself
in want, uncertainty.
What we call time
Is perhaps finally to give up!
I forget His name!
I forget how I wailed
With desire, tired in the morning light!
Now the Suitors devastate the house.
I forget! I forget
His name!
War corrupts.
Memory diminishes.
To besiege or be besieged
Is the same thing in the end. But
like spilled-out water to deny oneself
An embrace? Oh if I could only glimpse
Your armour in the crowd!

3.

Bones hair feathers scales!
The years pass gaily and evening draws in
Inviolable are the minerals' laws caking
The earth, the gaudy surfaces are flaking:
Over the unattended face that was sleep's
Over the unattended face that was the dream's
Unattended mask

4.

A body is to bear a shrine
Of relics, bones like porcelain
I am not yet an old
Woman, it distresses me!
I am weaving a web. I dreamed
Last night of a vessel drifting
Towards a far-off shore
Do you remember me? The one who
Returns is always another
With a forehead marked by war's shadow,
And a body engraved with the scars
Of all that is not its own!
Who returns the person one was?
What one has lost is real:
What one has lost one has
And retains forever. A waiting,
A Man. Do You remember me?
Hurry, if You can.

IV

*'For there is no place that does not
see you. You must change your life.'*

RAINER MARIA RILKE

1

Come home from the dark waters
Come home from out of the gale
Like a first-former with your red
schoolbag on your back, come
home. Confusing what
was, confusing you.
The days look like one another.
Rows of jars filled with blood and mucus.
It's a question of not remembering
It's a question of not remembering that morning
down by the shiny water, real
as an imagining!
Once upon a time there was innocence and pleasure
Once upon a time there was a reckless purity
One is a moment
One is a floor of sand in the market tent
One ferries small children and ice-skates
to and fro along slippery winter roads in one's yearning
for the cool light, come home

2

There is a despair
so great that it cannot be seen: a smoke
in our breath on cold days, a
weariness, a dream of surrender
It merges with the water's cycle
that holds our bodies captive
It occupies our memories and returns
its inventories in unrecognisable form
Its victims oppose
rescue. Its sign is want
It lacks gestures or
written signs: shells of small creatures
stratified to limestone.

There is a despair as inescapable
as ice, the fishes' white-shimmering sky.

3

In order to destroy those we love
we dress them up as fools in the
Nocturnal Theatre. And they rise in revolt!
We stand there like clowns ourselves!
Masked into dream they were even more
themselves. Tender-footed felines. Strong,
uncorrupted. They are going to deceive us.
That which we call time deceives us.
I myself for example am the sort of person
who continues to wander up and down
the short familiar stretch between high-rise blocks
with the too-difficult music in my bag and
an objective, growing despair at
being myself. At not being able to be someone
else. It is October with metallic
air, metallic sky and the banished
loved ones who walk with us in the smoke
of our breath. We look at them,
we must never lose them again.

4

I see you in the slow night.
There is a scent of water and bird-cherry.
Hair is coming loose in drifts on the sheet,
perhaps it will regenerate itself, it doesn't
matter, but it is coming loose.
I know how to handle the simpler
firearms, it doesn't help me.
I lack sexual imagination.
One buys something in ready-made parts
and they won't fit together.
One lets oneself be covered in
mud and the nausea of Grief.
But I don't want to be among these nights'
Emergency vehicles, shapes floating across
the water-damaged mirror, the waste
from the immense slaughterhouses!
Bird-cherry blossoms in the vase, drops vermin
over the tablecloth's blue embroideries of care.
A texture falls apart.
I lack sexual imagination, the bodies
that poured the secretion of their terrible
tenderness into each other. Oh, is there
anywhere that does not see you?
The night scrapes at the skeleton.
A texture slowly falls apart:
without the hope that is memory
we would not exist.

5

As in a mirror
the light images float by:
little girls with pigtails walk here
along the garden streets, frail
old ladies. One looks round for
one's lover, that was another time.
The temperature varies here.
One converses politely:
'I'd appreciate a bit less
speed', 'If necessary I shall have to kill you'
But how is one to know what's rubbish?
What's broken and what is without flaws?
Forget everything that hurt you so much.
You are going to be tortured like a feathered
caress, you are going to be tortured to
a gall-burst fish, you are going to be tortured
to darkness dissolved in darkness.

6

The works hotel turns out to be
a nocturnal construction of rotten
wood gleaming against the black verdure
There is an odour of lakewater
and August. Not a soul
in sight
So one must sleep here
So one must read some books,
take one's medicine and sleep
Instead I dream of the face
that splits open in bleeding
fissures
'You are time that must be whiled away'
A window stands barely open on the night
A window stands barely open on the morning light,
someone is raking gravel and singing The Trout,
in the town across the bay a bus is starting up.
And I don't even know whether I have been alone.

7

Sometimes visitors
are appalled by the house's seclusion,
the green darkness under the trees.
But I do have the main road!
Itinerant companies while away
the days with merry pranks
The dead and maimed are ferried
to and fro on carts during the night
The dwarfs grin and try to
creep in under my skirts
It never gets really lonely here
Just as long as I have the main road!

8

As in prayer
a little girl stands still
with raised hands
in the water, swims out. So our summers
go by: in the shadow beneath tall
trees, and the other bank in sunlight.
The smoke from the sauna wanders strangely
along the slope
A mist drifts across the water:
The one you are waiting for will not arrive
The one you are waiting for is travelling elsewhere
Dew is falling, the apples are falling
A girl is still playing on the riverbank
as if she were little
'But can't you see? It's me!'
It starts to snow violently:
We take place at unknown depths
in insufficient light, but even what
can be seen is beautiful.
The cracks, the water. Vessels
of fever and salt.

It was the hottest day of the summer.
We walked down by the water, and you
who have become my brother-and-sister talked about
someone who had fallen ill, football matches,
Thelonius Monk and the factory
you had visited in your dream, familiar
and different for each person
You said that nothing is ever finished
You said that everything is transitory

except for a few glowing
and soiled pictures that are sorrow, that
are the sorrow that flows through
friendship like water,

a few over-exposed sequences that
we press ashamedly to our hearts.